73

Thin Ice Olympics

by Jeffrey McDaniel

Write Bloody Publishing

writebloody.com

First edition.
ISBN: 978-1949342437

Cover Design by Angelo Maneage
Interior Layout by Nikki Steele
Edited by Kendra DeColo
Proofread by Alex Wolfe
Author Photo by Caroline Kaye

Type set in Bergamo.

Printed in the USA

Write Bloody Publishing
Los Angeles, CA

Support Independent Presses
writebloody.com

"The caution of a fox walking over ice is proverbial…. His ears constantly alert to the cracking of the ice, as he carefully and circumspectly searches out the safest spots."

—Hexagram #64, Before Completion, I Ching

THIN ICE OLYMPICS

Table of Contents

ONE MAN GRIND

Here I am: one man
all by his lonesome
on a dance floor
the size of a cruise ship
shaking his moneymaker
under imaginary stars.
Just one man
getting his fake groove on
all by his lonesome,
making sweet love
to the perfumed silence,
spitting kisses into the throat
of the brown-eyed wind.

The Beach

A friend said *have fun at the beach*, and she meant it derisively. Like I was
skipping off with a picnic basket of nothing burgers. *The beach* does imply
relaxation, a letting go. But it's also where land and water meet, where
civilization ends. The liquid lifts and curls and crashes—a repetitive
message, but from whom? And all that sky, unimpeded, besides the
occasional plane dragging a banner for *one-dollar tacos at Ron's*. And all
the memories washing onto the shore of your mind. The brain's frothy,
flooded basement flinging things up, like your dead father, or a love story
from years ago.

The beach is a psychiatrist's sofa inside a holy space, with the walls and
ceiling ripped off. A salty hint of danger always in the air. Less than a
month ago, on this beach, a fifteen-year-old boy was sucked away by the
waves and taken where exactly? Lifeguards formed a human chain and
combed the ocean's unruly hair and found nothing. Days later the ocean
shouldered him back onto shore.

When I stand at the water's edge with my twelve-year-old daughter,
is it really just *a day at the beach*? To my right: the bell tower of a hotel I
stayed at with my father fifty years ago, him tossing me in the air in the
hotel pool. I turn and visualize him on this very sand, five years ago,
with a portable oxygen tank slung over his shoulder. The wave slaps the
shoreline: the earth's truest clock. Is it just *a day at the beach*, if I needed to
come here to feel his presence? Just *a day at the beach*, if this is the only
place my daughter will really talk to me? The words flow when our feet
are in the foam, tossing a ball back and forth, like my father did with me.
She lifts above the confines of the present, possibility expands: *Do you
think I'll make JV? Can you believe...* Here the future is laid out in front of
us. Or is it the past? I guess it depends on your age and what you packed
in your beach bag.

The morning my father died two years ago, I woke near the beach in the
state of his birth. I walked the April shoreline, and this will sound absurd,
but I watched his spirit climb, a spiral vapor trail, into the sky.

If you are grieving, I tell you: go to the beach. The salt water will open
the pores of your soul. Yes, the beach is where you hit the volleyball,
dolphin over waves, ride bikes on the boardwalk with your kid, but it's
also where you see your dead father standing in the sand in his Panama
hat and trousers, where you hear his crusty voice and remember how he
paid some guy at the hotel twenty bucks to park his car.

Autumn Oak

After hours of rain and a drain-pipe rattling wind
that forty-foot stud in the front yard quivers,

a yellow shirt scattered at his feet. Look
at those skinny limbs. Where did the day go?

This morning I was ten and rolling down the slope
of my grandmother's lawn, then twelve in my bedroom,

a pillow over my head, then fourteen and peering out
a dark window at a neighbor in her bathrobe.

Now I'm brushing the smell of middle age
from my teeth. *Next train for Youth and Imagination*

departing in five minutes, the conductor barks,
his voice: a stack of birth certificates being fed

into a paper shredder. Off I march into my sad excuse
for a time machine. Now I'm eating Brussels sprouts,

fried calamari at a friend's fiftieth. The wind has peeled
off the front yard stud's leafy pants. He's down

to his yellow boxers, flickering in the moonlight.

November Red-Eye with Dead Childhood Friends

Can't sleep on the red-eye from Los Angeles.
My thirteen-year-old snoozes on the folded-out

food tray. I click on *The Shining*. The death march
synthesizer as Jack and Shelly drive with little Danny

in their yellow Bug up a two-lane mountain road
to—wait, false alarm—it's Jack going solo

to the job interview. The suits are so '70's polyester.
At sixteen, I watched this movie with Drew

on a thirteen-inch Sony in his mom's bedroom.
He was tripping on acid and his forehead percolated

with sweat. My daughter pops up—blood gushes
from the elevator doors—luckily she has an eye mask on.

I wince and watch Jack flush five months of sobriety
with a shot of whisky. Creigh's funeral launches

in thirty-two hours. I will twirl the eulogy
and throw it like a giant lasso and corral the hearts

of his parents in the front row. *Honey, I'm home,* Jack says,
his ax bashing through the bathroom door. That's how I'd look

if I wasn't sober. My daughter takes photos
of the white carpet beneath the airplane's wing.

Inside the white fabric, my dead childhood friends play
hide and seek, with chunks of broken glass for teeth.

Diabetes

At a middle-aged party, watching housewives
dance on a patterned living room rug, taking tugs

off a Juul, I consider what the doctor said the day before:
Die. You will die. Parts of you are dying right now,

and my six dead friends come back to life and take turns
staring at me from an orange chair across the room.

You will die one beat at a time. No sugar. No bread.
No palmfuls of candy crammed in my mouth.

*You will know the difference between hunger
and emptiness.* But why is the third syllable so easy,

I wonder. First you *die*, then you get *beat*, then you slide
on the icy *eee's*. I will beat this, I wince.

Even as I say farewell to my old friends:
Skittles, Gatorade, blood-colored licorice. Adios,

three bowls of midnight Honey Nut Cheerios.
No more shoveling you down, small bowling ball

of pulverized oats, hugging me from the inside.
Back at the party, one of the glossy Sirens beckons me

to dance, her hands like sopaipillas covered in honey.

NOTES ON MIRO'S *THE BIRTH OF THE WORLD*

Was he perturbed, flinging paint at the canvas? Do we even know each other? Are you an exchange student from the Czech Republic with a streak of blue in your hair, or are you some faint, watered-down version of my mother? There are splotches of black, the same color as the bags under her eyes. I heard Gucci is making bags under people's eyes. Designer drugs equal designer problems. Last week a doctor told me I had *diabetes*, the first syllable echoing in my head.

There's a black spider web in the bottom left corner, or is it thirty percent of a wheel? The white circle is not a moon. It's the head of a person. And the white string coming out of the moon-head is the torso and neck combined, and then we see his waist, and he's kneeling on one knee, his left knee extended—proposing to someone who didn't make it into the painting. He's kneeling on the string of the red balloon he will use to levitate out of the frame if the special someone says no.

In the upper right corner, the black blurs with the gray and it looks like a sky, with squiggly blue lines. If the black is a cloud, then the blue lines are rain. But since when is rain blue? Are you rain or are you the teardrops of a black hole? Maybe this painting is how babies are made, like the painting happens in a pre-life space, and the red balloon is what the formulating human will use to rise out of the oily womb and enter the world.

Inquiring Minds

People want to know how I got so fat. The truth is
it wasn't easy. It took a serious commitment.

A lot of late nights. Dedication. Persistence.
Hitting the fridge when other people were sleeping.

I just wanted that three a.m. cereal more. I gritted
through the gut pain and the humiliation

of yet another pair of pants seam-ripping. I sucked
in my stomach to get the zipper up, ignored the red

calligraphy on my waist. My daughter charging in
and snatching soda from the table. But *why,*

people ask. The truth is I was auditioning
for a movie, *The Glutton,* and it would be more authentic

if I put on fifty pounds. Kind of like *The Joker,*
but with food, and Christian Bale was unavailable.

I sacrificed my looks and physique in the name of art.
But *why,* people ask. The truth is I pounded

all those double-doubles, guzzled all those sugar drinks
as part of a monogamy enhancement experiment.

But *why?* I was building a space suit of shame
one candy bar wrapper at a time. It kept me grounded

on Earth. But *why?* Because I was afraid
of being an astronaut. Because I'm a creature

of habit. Because I didn't want to feel.
Because I like going to sleep with a cannonball

of dough in my belly. Because I wanted to see
what it feels like to be fucked from the inside.

Because it took on a life of its own. Because
I couldn't tell the difference between life and art.

PHANTOM BIRTH

I lost my father figure and my father two months apart. Two deathbeds in one season. Four on-the-brink eyes. It's 10:29 a.m. March 1st. Would be my dad's eighty-second. (Cue in the violins and wet eyes close-up.) No wonder I've been playing dodgeball with reality since midnight. *What are we running from,* I ask my anti-self. When you're running is not the best time to answer that question. Like asking *why* as the pills are dropping down the elevator shaft of the throat and a hundred tiny piano players are unleashed in your bloodstream. Why don't our feet bulge with blood like plastic bags filled with red water? My penis feels beat-up. Not like it's been in a fight, but like it got pounded on. (Excuse me, Mr. Author, but the testicles have a lot more in common visually with a punching bag, the way they hang down etc.) The new Diabetes medicine makes each bowel movement feel like a total evacuation. The new diet feels like a permanent state of fasting. My stomach feels like a one-room apartment that has not been moved into yet. My eyes feel like—(Quick, cut to the eyes. He sparred incessantly with his dad. Why all the belly aching? Also, he wrote about his dad in his last book. Is he trying to build a hotel on one of the islands of grief? Time to go back to the mainland and stick with the living.) The wind howls the gap between the red front door and the white frame. It's been a warm winter, one cock of snow. (Um, last I checked a cock was not a unit of measure. And whose cock are we using. Fact-check, please.) But now it's the first of March. The flowers long, slow march up and out of the earth. The thing is: I just wanted to connect who I am now with who I was as a kid. My dad and I were blissfully close until I was eight and I just wanted to experience that closeness on the other side of the river, so my life made sense. It feels like our almost-mythic closeness exists on some island that has been sucked down and preserved in the earth's bowels, a personalized Atlantis. Of course, I'm to blame—I growled *fuck you* at him seven hundred forty-six times. We only approached our mythic closeness twice in the last forty years: the night I was on heroin and woke him at 3:00 a.m. and coaxed him into the living room, where we smoked hash, and he was covered in the residue of dream and a hundred percent his old, gentle self, and the day before he died, on his good-bye bed, when I spoke to him for several hours, my hand on his chest, telling him every single thing he needed to hear. Why is this ending now? Because I can't bear to write another word.

FIRST DAYS OF SPRING

You're in your driveway. The sun
opening its almost liquid arms over the lawn
and asphalt where you stand. *Thank you*
you say to the two guys in orange vests,
gripping your trash can with gloved hands,
dumping a week's worth of Pellegrino bottles,
milk cartons, cursed newspapers, ripped
leaf bags, four-color mailers for Broadway shows
no one will ever see into the masher. *Thank you*
you say again, your voice rising a notch
on the octave ladder, the two most sincere words
you've uttered all year. *Thank you*
you want to cry from the papier-mâché roof
of your lungs, as the truck groans to the house
next door, where your neighbor was wheeled out
into an ambulance seventeen hours ago
by emergency workers in white masks,
like cloth hands cupped over their mouths,
their clenched eyes the only things vaguely face-like
about their faces. *Thank you*, you want to yell
to the grocery store workers two blocks away
from the lip of your property, the island of soil
you and your family survive on, the sun
crashing in waves on the black shore.

Corona Theme Song

Bela Lugosi's Dead is the only song that makes sense
you think while scooping shriveled autumn leaves

into an un-crumpled brown paper leaf bag on a March day
so windy the leaves blow from the rake's bony hand.

The rake is the hand of death in this equation. *Undead,*
undead repeating in your ears. The jittery chime guitar

like the amplified chattering of a meth fiend's teeth.
Death looks at your white mask and smirks. *The bats*

have indeed *left the bell tower,* you think, as you eyeball
the house fifty feet away, where the father

was carted off to ventilator-land three days ago. Cut
to Death jaunting down a throbbing underground hallway.

Of course, mirrored sunglasses. Of course, sour milk skin.
Lips red as the last person's neck slit open.

Where is Catherine Deneuve when you need her?
The awful March sun stamping its yellow finger on that house.

HOLDING UP

How you holding up?
High waves of anxiety
mixed with periods of surface calm.

How you holding up?
By a thread. I'm being held up
by a single thread and what scares me
is not knowing what's inside
the liquid I'm being held up over
and is it cold?

How you holding up?
With both hands. I'm holding it up
with both hands.

How you holding up?
Like a bank with Monopoly money in the drawers.
Like a three-day-old birthday cake.
Like a middle finger out a car window.
Like a bad perm on a rainy day.
Like the hand of a mediocre student in the back row
who wants to show he's participating
but doesn't want to get called on.
Like the eyebrows of Winona Ryder.
Like a fist from a pile of rubble.

Surefire

I stick my finger in the dictionary and touch a word
surefire: certain to succeed. Next door neighbor

to *surefooted.* Good neighbors for sure, the biggest
house on the block. No one is borrowing sugar.

No one is stepping on the porch. Good fences
make good barriers to hide behind as your neighbors

straighten their ties and adjust their makeup
in the April rain. T.S. Eliot was right. April

is the Genghis Khan of months. Hear that sound?
Me either. That is not the sound of the father's car door

closing and pulling out of the driveway at six a.m.
That is not the sound of him clapping

at his kid's basketball game. *Good-bye, dad,*
they say. *Good luck on your trip, your journey,*

as they lower his body into the submarine
built for one. The mourners, you ask?

Oh, they were the ones in parked cars,
holding balloons and flowers and signs

out of rolled-down car windows, as the rain
came down like nails from a roofer's gun.

WHEN THE CAT'S AWAY

When the cat's away, the mice
will slip on party hats
and sneak into the liquor cabinet.
When the cows are away,
the milk bucket will bathe
in moonlight. *Little pitchers have large ears,*
said the mother pointing at the ceiling.
Little silences have big echoes,
said the stoned composer.
Little kisses have a way of growing
into big penises, said the grandmother
on prom night. *Little leaks sink a ship,*
yelled the captain, seawater on his lips.
A little knowledge is a dangerous dress
to wear to a night club, said the father
in little socks. *Little strokes fell great oaks,*
said the papercut lashing
into your finger. *Little things*
please little minds, said the pervert
staring at himself in the mirror.
Little thieves are hanged, but big thieves escape,
cackled Creigh, as my younger brothers
were whisked away in the paddy wagon.

TWENTY-SEVEN DAYS AND COUNTING

You're taking a walk, and it's thirty-six degrees outside.
Your socks go up to your ankles. More like fabric canoes

than socks. The moon is low and white
and looks like someone took a bite out of it.

This will be known as the year humanity
had a bite taken out of its neck. No necking

at the prom this spring. What's a handshake,
Junior will ask in ten years. The cement of trust,

you'll respond. What's a tongue kiss, he'll ask.
That was when we closed our eyes and went swimming

in the ocean of another person's mouth. Junior
will adjust his Spiderman face shield, except

you're actually all alone in a one-room apartment
for twenty-seven days and counting.

POWER OUTAGE

The wind, ballistic in the branches, rakes
the asbestos siding. Plastic trash cans

rattle the driveway. Electricity sucked
from the wires like bionic lemonade.

The food in the fridge is golden
for four hours. Let's kill the milk.

It's gonna die anyway. *But what about the cow,*
says the pound of sirloin, dying

again on the meat shelf. Suddenly voltage
surges and voila—the stove blinks 3:43.

Why bother re-setting? A dad texts you
photos of a wall calendar he's been using

as a semen landing pad: yellowing blasts
of potential humans stretching out

across the blank days of April. *Time
is fucking me, so I'm fucking it back.*

The Difference between Right and Wrong

Bladder is a weird word for where the urine
gets stored. It's just a holding station. A malleable flask.

Also, has taking a number two ever reminded you
of that scene in an action flick, when the belly

of the military plane opens and the soldiers
Geronimo out? Me either. But wouldn't it be cool

if each launched turd had a tiny white parachute
that bloomed upon descent into the basin. And hair?

Is there a little farmer between the ribs who grows it,
then ships it to different parts of the body?

Take this up to the scalp, boss. And these tiny threads
to the arms and legs. And this coarser stuff to the pits.

And this fine batch down to the gennies. And these loose strands
to the knuckles. And this woven scarf to the brows.

If not, then where does hair come from? Case in point:
the forearm. Are there hair seeds, pre-planted in strips,

that emerge when a person screeches into puberty?
And don't even get me started on the mysteries of breast milk.

Remember that scene at the end of *The Grapes of Wrath*,
where that lady breast feeds the starving man?

Some kid in seventh grade convinced me the title
referred to a starving man's testicles. *The balls shrivel*

when you don't eat. The balls are the first to go. Of course,
that evening I went on a secret hunger strike.

But after twenty-three hours my hairless walnuts
were the same .73 pounds when I late-night lowered them

onto the family scale, placed strategically on the kitchen table.
What are you doing down there, my father yelled.

Just getting a cookie, I yelled back. *But why did you bring the scale,*
he asked. *Just trying to tell the difference between right and wrong*, I said.

Ok, he said, hugging me at the top of the stairs,
muffling a sob into my shoulder.

poem that begins with a bad juvenile joke

What happens when an administrator takes a poop?
 I don't know.
A bureaucrap.
 That's not even funny.
Yeah, but your face buried under that thundercloud is.
 Is today take your inner-middle-schooler to quarantine day?
I'm not doing well.
 Did you get enough sleep?
No.
 Did you put your brain and all your thoughts and muscles and internal
 organs into the dishwasher of sleep for the long or short cycle?
I washed my thoughts by hand. Rinsed them one-
by-one through the soapy water and sang happy
birthday to myself.
 Is today your birthday?
I want to celebrate every day like it could be my last.
 Are you sad?
No.
 Are your shoulders sandbags and is a foggy moisture accumulating
 behind your eyes?
Yes.
 Are you angry?
No.
 Are you a great wind blowing dead leaves and ripped pieces of paper?
Yes.
 Are you anxious?
No, I'm the one gathering up the leaves and ripped pieces of paper
and taping them back together.
 Are you Sisyphus?
Yes, except I am not allowed outside to climb the mountain today,
and my rock is sitting in the driveway, like a tired, granite dog.

Good Day

Unload the bikes from the rack.
Only eight hundred Americans dead so far today.
A cardinal flutters from a tree's green dress.
Children are losing feeling in their toes.
The sun is a patient father.
Russian doctors keep falling from windows.
Your wife and daughter pedal ahead
     on the gravel path.
The sense of smell evaporates
     like a red popsicle dropped on pavement.
A lazy creek runs alongside the bike path.
No ambulances on your street in at least a week.
Cows munching grass in the valley.
You adjust your mask and pedal harder
     into what feels like a good day.

WREN

for Camilla Wren McDaniel

Between your first and last names
there's an opening you can slide through,
a four-letter blouse we stitched
and hung in your closet, a lone syllable
planted at birth. It's perched
on a branch, a feathery escape valve.
You can slip into it and fly to the forest,
the city, wherever you need, leave
the rolling hills of your old syllables behind.

THE HABER PROCESS

Humans water each other with their eyes.
  That's a touchy-feely image and it doesn't hold water.
Pun much?
  I'm the Christopher Columbus of puns—I land on them
  when looking for something else. But what I mean is
  you're implying, in this time of Isolation, we're missing
  something fundamental, that we need sunshine
  and water to grow. Both real and metaphorical.
  I concur, but are "eyes" more like water or more like the sun
  in this context? You said "water," but "water" paired with "eyes"
  is overused, suggests crying, whether you meant that or not.
  "Sunlight" is the more accurate image—warmth, beaming etc.
What about carbon? Isn't that more
like what eyes do? Isn't carbon
closer to love? You can't see it
but it's all around you, always
touching you, protecting you
like you're surrounded
by crunchy love particles.
  No, love is more like a nutrient. Love is the soil
  that a person grows out of. Love is the dirt
  filled with potassium and earthworms and sulfur.
No, love is more like nitrogen,
  Yeah, if you're a terrorist building bombs.
Bombs are only one use of nitrogen.
You can use it to make fertilizer and dyes and—
  Bombs, jackass. Nitrogen is like a boring ass white girl:
  transparent, no smell, acting all pure,
  but mix it with hydrogen and it will give you—
Amnesia. It will make you forget
the most important aspect of love: you must let go
of the other person's shortcomings.
  That's not love. That's devotion. You been huffing
  ammonia? Ever hear of the Texas City Disaster?
  1947. Galveston Bay. Twenty-two-hundred tons
  of ammonium nitrate, on a boat. "Why
  is the water boiling," a bystander asked,
  pointing at the harbor. The deck beginning to bulge
  with expanding steam and Ka-Boom—

a thousand buildings smithereened. Bales
of burning twine propelled into the sky,
then plummeted back to earth, like the flaming hair
of Salem witches. An airplane's wings
shaved clean off. Thirty firemen dead. Windows
shattered ten miles away. Six thousand tons
of steel pirouetting through the air.
That's exactly the kind of love I'm talking about.

Just Woke and Already Tired

Chivalry is aiming your morning pee
at the side of the porcelain basin

to spare your cohabitants
the chainsaw hum. It's sixty degrees.

This is the year we all lived like Emily
Dickinson. *You can't wear that sweater—*

look at the pilling. Not with your beard.
You look like a homeless person.

You can't go out in pajamas. I'm listening
to the singing of a man who plunged

a steak knife into his own chest. The blanket
of clouds is unmoved. Two months in

and the hounds are barking slurs
up the old flagpoles. Two months

and already our roots are showing through
two-toned, two-faced, too afraid. Barely noon

and I've already burned the one card
up my sleeve: forest bathing. A neighbor

leans out her second-floor window
and paints the side of her house,

like trying to apply suntan lotion
to the center of your back. My frontal

lobe throbs. My brain is a toy bomb
being passed in a circle by invisible kids.

The cave parts of my body suddenly bristle.
This is the year spouses became barbers.

In college I got away with the same socks
and boxers for three days. Now I'm fifty-two

and wishing the shower was a slow-motion
fire hose held by God.

FACTS

You think because you grew up
in a progressive neighborhood
in a racist city, a few years after
the Civil Rights Movement
you are somehow immune? You think
because you had a Black swim coach
and pedaled your dirt bike to practice
through a West Philly color line
and fell in love with rap music
and taught yourself to pop at fourteen
that you get a pass? Your skin
has a membership card
woven into the pores. Your Band-Aid
colored skin. Your front-of-the-bus skin.
Your skin that is such a secret handshake
you don't even have to lift your hands.
Your stars-on-the-flag skin.
Your tiny-lie-colored skin.
Your smile-as-you-enter-the-store skin.
Your how-fast-was-I-going-sir skin.
Your jogging-in-peace skin.

WILLIAM (BARR)

Barring any unforeseen Friday night circumcisions
    on democracy's genitalia,
a barrage of pepper spray up the Statue of Liberty's robe.
Barracudas in tuxedos and urine on tombstones.
His face a sagging beige bucket with eye slits and a barf bag.
In khaki shorts, bumbling barefooted on a street with Adam's apples
    for cobblestones,
an eroded barnacle in his bright white underpants.
Future historians will scrape the barren ventricles
    of his battleship heart.
Hail the castrated baritone.
Hail the barbed wire of his lips
in his barracks on a mattress of trick Bibles.
The barrel of laughs evaporates when he steps in the room.
Embarrassed colleagues cover their eyes
as he fills the wheelbarrow with lies.
His threadbare conscience.
His constitutional barbarisms
under a sybaritic moon.

SCREWDRIVER ON THE HUDSON

8:16 a.m. An invisible screwdriver
burrows an inch above your eyes.

Consider yourself lucky. Symmetrical
headaches are much easier to diffuse.

Several hours north of here, your daughter
just woke in the highest branches

of a pine tree. She and ten basketball teammates
are roasting the eyes of future misogynists

over an open flame. They're juggling
ax handles and kayaking across a lake

of liquid glass. If you listen closely,
you can hear the old man in overalls

making his morning rounds, unhooking
the stars he hammered into place

twelve hours before. Not a bad job. South of here,
on the northern fringes of the city, the swimming

pools: closed. The basketball rims: unscrewed
from the backboard. But the cardinals,

worms and hummingbirds are still employed,
doing their essential, primordial work.

speak not of my debts unless you mean to pay them

The faint pulse of a lymph node
A head of biological confetti
A cigarette stubbed out in one nostril
A skyscraper of meth in the other
An ice cube figure-skating on a nipple
The penis hopping out of bed
The kneecaps melting under time's glare
A lung full of spider webs
A toxic spill in your briefs
Shadows tiptoeing your periphery
A scrub brush growing from your face
A burb percolating in your throat
Knuckles wishing they were egg shells
An orgasm running off the penis's diving board
    and covering its eyes as it hovers in the air
      for what feels like an eternity before it shatters
      the calendar's still water with a splash

THE UNSCREWING

Make a list of all the people you've had sex with
and then count how many you would unscrew

if you had the chance. Better yet—how many
entanglings would you dismantle

and re-screw properly? You were a novice
putting together an Ikea cabinet. No clue

how to hold a hinge and done too quickly.
What did you know about touch, about reading

into the complexity of sensation, turning
each page of skin, reading every sentence over

and over, until her spine arches and sighs
ricochet off the ceiling? You know

for such a two-timing hoe you really
weren't that good in bed. The worst

of both worlds. If you're going to be a hoe,
at least do your homework, be a hoe

with commitment. Not a halfway hoe
barreling through foreplay like a rush-hour

subway station, as if there was somewhere
more important you needed to be.

Debt

You will pay for this one day, the sky whispered.
You will pay for your sins in a currency that hasn't been printed yet.
You will pay in nickels of blood, quarters of breath.
You will pay in chipped marble chunks of your soul.
You will pay through the gut for what you did/said/thought.

But when will my debt be paid, I asked.
When you stop borrowing in the groin of the night,
you furry ingrate. And with that cannon blast of clarity
I start my day, like the engine of a freshly washed car
always on the verge of being paid off.

ELEGY FOR A ROTTEN TOOTH

Imagine an orange slice, freshly cut. Lift it
to your lips and chomp—fireworks of citrus bloom
over your buds. Now imagine
a pinprick-wide hole, buried under a filling
in your lower left molar. Imagine the gush
of orange juiciness, a bevy of droplets trickling
down and square on the nerve, now throbbing
in the gum pulp, like the cock of a pervert
with a foot fetish, leering from his basement window
at the parade of flip-flops on a July morning.
Imagine your neck veins yanking like ropes,
as a tiny drunk piano player goes full death fugue
on your splendid eighty-eights.

THIRTY YEARS LATER

I don't kiss anyone, I fuck, she says—
those six words, a leather boot kicking
a hole in the dream you hoped
would end with making out. The end
of the dream is a drag: stuck
across from her at a six-top
in a fancy restaurant. Spouses
in the mist. You sneak off to text her:
you want to hung. A dozen times
you type *hang* wrong. Groggy
on your real-life couch, you rub
the dream from your eyes, google
her first name + "homeopathy"
+ the city she lives in, and her face
pops up: a stranger with firm, faded
blue eyes, a well-adjusted smile,
soap commercial teeth. Do not
schedule an appointment and ask her
to listen to the murmur in your heart.
Close the window. Let the sun be the one
to kiss light into her hair.

September 18th

The first leaf parachutes from the bough. The softest ax blade
on the throat of summer. Some leaves don't give up

so easy. Ruth Bader Ginsburg grips the branch. Last night
in Los Angeles the earth shook, a cosmic alarm clock,

even as the hills burned, even as a mist floated between mouths
at frat parties. And the fire hoses are filled with kerosene.

Justice is a tortoise eating strawberries from a silver bowl,
its neck jabbing like an arm, its mouth a boxer's fist

punching the food, pummeling what it wants. Democracy
is an unmarked car, a pale goon, with formaldehyde for saliva,

a game of Three-card Monte in broad daylight.

PRISONS OF THE FUTURE

will have no walls—just an electric fence
with tiny lightning bolts reverberating
up wayward prisoners' calves. Clones
in the watch tower. Drones serving dregs
and donuts. Cots under open-air tents
with infrared heat lamps. Let them
walk free. Let them exercise the muscles
of autonomy. It's not prison. It's containment.
Air drop drugs and junk food.
Let them do their nightly Gaza Striptease.
If they breach the sizzling barricade,
send in the eight-foot-tall T-Rexes
and vampire clones—cops,
with capes and syringes for teeth—
who suck blood straight from the neck
and belly store it, while injecting
two days' worth of Valium to sing
those dreams of insurrection to sleep.

poem that starts somewhere gross, but doesn't end there

Covid has taught us that what we can't see is just as important as what we
    can.

Never leave your toothbrush in the same room as a toilet, or inevitably
    excrement molecules will infiltrate the air and land on the
    bristles and you will give yourself shit teeth.

What do you think about the whole spray chemical flowers in the
    bathroom after you take a grumpy? Do you think Walt Whitman
    would do that? If the scent of his armpits was an *aroma finer than
    prayer*, then what about the holy fragrance of a beef stew dookie?

Which American poets do you think grab the aerosol and eradicate
    the grimacing richness? Which American poets cannot handle the
    pugnacious onslaught of their own humanity?

Or do we imagine that certain American poets spray out of kindness for
    others? Kind of like wearing a mask.

Does anyone who lives alone attack the stench with an artificial spray?
    That seems a little much. If you can't handle your own shit, then
    what can you handle? Or maybe it's a smart move to prevent
    nostril fatigue.

I like to leave the window or door open and let the bathroom air out on
    its own schedule.

I'm neglecting the primordial power of sulfur, which reminds me of my
    dad and walking into his bathroom as a kid.

Do you ever feel like someone is lying to you when you enter right after
    them and catch a whiff of struck matches or chemical carnations?
    You know that stinky smell is in there, but it's hiding under a
    sulfur blanket. Would you rather just smell the real thing?

My dad started spending a lot of time in the bathroom when I was ten.
He was a good dad for the most part. It took a few years for me
to realize what he was doing in there: chain-smoking Belairs and
vanishing into a glossy rabbit hole, while ten-year-old me knocked
on the door. "Come on, dad. Let's go to the park."

*Give the old man a break—his wife was zonked out on Valium. At least he went
to work each day. The bathroom was a tiled confessional where he
yanked the truth out of himself and showed a little palmful to God.*

And God said: I don't forgive you.

Fire Pit for One

I'm alone at the fire pit. 12:12 a.m. A train running away from something in the distance. Fifty-nine degrees. The crickets sing, but not with enthusiasm. The up-lighting we added looks halfway decent. The pit throws up a spark that gets swallowed by the dark. One log resists. All the lamps in the house clicked off. Remember that girl in college who wore the gray negligee? The bazookas of her nipples. It was only a third of a century ago. The heat from the pit goes up the leg of my pants. Old men should unplug their desire and take out their earrings. Old men should put away their heat lamps. Yes, Santa Claus carries a big bag of toys, but what does October carry? October used to carry a big bag of candy. But now it's either carrying a vaccine or ground-up owls who died by the river. Somebody is bringing us something, but we don't know if it's good or bad. This is the year of the Etch A Sketch calendar. Halloween masks every day, but no Snickers. I'm that sad kind of person who goes to the beach even when it's too cold to swim. Always trying to get into the pants of the girl from the summer before. Always wanting one more of everything. One more log in the fire. One more bowl of cereal. One more cup of tea. One more sunset. Earlier, when people were here, a friend talked about her old neighbor, a Quaker, how he used to walk into her house unannounced and she would be in the kitchen in a bathrobe, and *he would just walk right in the back door*, and we all laughed. Do you think anyone has a revolving door on the back of their house? Do you think anyone has a spiral staircase inside their underpants? And what's so special about the back door anyway? Is it my imagination or did the crickets just get louder? Is it my imagination, or did the train just burrow under the Hudson and disappear into the year I was sleeping with a Republican? Is it my imagination, or is Dracula the president of America? Is it my imagination, or are the logs face down on the embers? Is it burning? It looks like it's just smoldering. But take the iron prong and flip the logs over and flames burst out. It's the same with art. So many people have the fire. They just don't know when to turn the seething logs.

Trump Rapper Names

Professor Grifter
Wigga Mortis (don't call me Morris)
Kublai Con
Big Daddy Covid (best believe I went viral)
Noose Wrld
Bougie Trash
I am Queens Boulevard
Gucci Crackers
45 Cray
Orange Lazarus
Putin's Stepchild
Tricky Dick (suck that)
Sir Jizz a Lot
Bizzy Resting
Fifth Avenue Killer (in broad daylight)
Ol' Dirty Dawg (count that money)
Pinocchio Dick (when I lie it gets bigger)
Invictus (bitches, leave you in stitches)
Graveyard 4 Truth
Permanent Midnight
Dim Reaper
Blinded by the Bling (kiss that ring)
Lucifer in Diapers
Oath Creeper
Pale-faced Honkee
Nazis are people too
Truth So Shall (grab that pussy)
De Mock Cray Tease
In So Wreck Shit

Pandemic Parable

In the second week of March 2020, C and I were in Costco, loading up on groceries and other provisions. It was days before what became the pandemic. The threats of supply chain shortages had people scurrying. Could turn out to be another Y2K. The toilet paper shelf was bare. Whole aisles ravaged. Our asses were out of luck. Literally. C stayed with the cart like a normal person. I scoured the aisles. Spied a stash of industrial toilet paper in the office supply section. *Marathon—value that goes the distance.* Snatched four large boxes, forty bucks each.

The pandemic turned out to be real, but not the toilet paper shortage. I felt like a fool, a hoarder. Four aquarium-tank sized boxes of jumbo-rolls in the basement. The paper was coarse. Gruff. Scruffy. Gritty. My wife and daughter refused to use it. The store wouldn't take it back. Could've just thrown it out. But that would've been wasteful. So I stocked it in the first-floor half-bathroom. My private tree-pulp-and-bleach cross to bear. My punishment for hoarding. Each agitating swipe: a reminder of my selfishness, my fear.

If my life was a Greek myth, then when I finished the twenty-four, nine-hundred-foot, two-ply gargantuan rolls—a full half-mile of ass wiping—the pandemic would be over. I powered through each scratchy swab, a modern-day Atlas with the fate of the world resting on my ass.

As fate would have it, I didn't catch Covid, until I was on the last roll. My head like slow-motion Jiffy Pop. Sweaty, kaleidoscopic thoughts. *Lightly-urinated-upon rug for sale.... Tomorrow is bring your rabbit hole to work day... Imagine if I take my last wipe on the same day my immunity system craps the last bit of the virus from its metaphorical bunghole... Imagine if I only live as long as the toilet paper supply lasts.* Imagine.

THE WORLD UNDERNEATH

You're in your backyard, laying out logs
for the sun to suck moisture from. Grunts and groans

from a truck on the street. A sawdust smell.
A touch of oil. A moth-eaten white rug being tugged

across the blue floor of the sky. Remember
ten years old, placing the square wall-mirror

on your scratchy red carpet, a new upside-down room
opening underneath? How you wanted to climb in,

walk on the ceiling. Your gravity-defying bunk bed,
the globe light centering the room. Tonight

the wood will catch quick and you and the fire pit crew
will recline and crackle in the world that opened

underneath our world, where children emerge
from the uterus, covered in hand sanitizer, wearing masks.

FUNERALS OF THE FUTURE

Womb-shaped coffins
for that elusive feeling of rebirth.
Pill bottle coffins.
Syringe coffins. Dildo coffins.
Mini Cadillac coffins to roll
mack daddy-style into the afterlife.
Why just a six-foot hole
with a priest lubing the soil?
Why not make the earth
look like a vein, or a mouth,
or a pulsating orifice? This
is eternity, people.

THE VASE

My mother told me
that when she dies
she wants to be enrolled
in a furnace
and turned into ash,
then she wants me
to leave the ash outside
in a big glass bowl
and let the rain
soak into it,
then me to stir it up
into a kind of clay,
make a vase out of it,
put it in a kiln,
and when I die,
have my ashes
placed inside,
so she can carry me
again, forever.

THE IN-BETWEEN

5:34 a.m. The plan was to just haul the cardboard box
the puppy crate came in to the curb, but the fifty-seven-degree

mid-October air pulls you up the street
in your lace-less yard sneakers, into the beginning of dawn.

Or is it the end of night? Your daughter upstairs in bed. Her ankle
swollen purple and black, a used ice pack on the wood floor,

as you waltz the in-between. The red light is on upstairs
in a neighbor's bedroom, where a twenty-year-old overdosed

five years ago. A car engine grinds—Jonno commencing
his fifty-mile slide to the city, where Covid stretches

its muscles for round two. The birds not singing.
Political signs wedged into the dirt. Recycling cans.

Streetlights on, murmuring dark. Scant Halloween decorations.
Eleven days away. No one's feeling it. Yesterday you woke

on a dirt floor with a shovel and dug deeper into the pit.
Then you slapped on your Dad hat and went to the doctor

with your daughter. The X-ray was the color of the sky,
and the doctor couldn't tell if it was night or morning. A tiny

growth plate fracture, or just a sprain? Is the sun rising
in three weeks or three months? The good news: you have work

in-person today—no moping around and blasting farts
into the pity pot. No stuffing your face with gloomy emotions.

You must move forward, with your deity, and let your daughter
study from home with hers. Sometimes under the same roof

the deities blur. A train horn blares twice by the river. A person
on the tracks, or just the iron beast being polite? Inside the train bathroom

a hidden bucket where urine sloshes. Thirty years ago
you didn't think walking could be part of your writing process.

A grayish-white light haunts the mountains. The humidity
doesn't let the light lift and expand. The clouds are parents

telling the light what it can and can't do. Your one parent
is in the soil. Your other parent is propped up

in a wheelchair. You got to stay scrappy. Whether thirteen
or fifty-three. You can unravel in your little pit

and try to escape with various shovels, one shaped like a spoon,
another shaped like your dick, but you still got to buck up,

strap on those little stilettos and march out of the house
and down this street where people are sleeping.

Take note of the sky. Wonder why the birds are still dreaming.
Take note of the tiny see-through ghost by the fire hydrant.

Your jangly shadow. The waist-high bag of leaves. Today
is going to be seventeen feet long. There will be curves.

Pace yourself, my friend. That stop sign right ahead of you—
what's on the other side? Trees? Heroin? Cracked-out nymphs

caroling: want to taste my rabbit hole? That stop sign
is not for you. You're not going over the guard rail

and into the forest. You're turning right, toward the house
with the dog, the child, the wife. In a few hours

you'll just be another car, barreling south to work,
but for now you're still human, holding a straw

and drinking the bruised purple light of dawn.

BEIGE HERO(IN) JULY

What was I thinking? That summer I wore combat boots
with the laces untied, like they were high-tops? No job,
a girlfriend in theory, but all the love leaked out, drug money
grifted from granny, me the favorite, eating egg sandwiches
from the Korean deli on 7th Avenue, waiting for the sun to fall
like the head of a French king into the Hudson, the nightly slide
to Alphabet City. What word was I trying to spell, slipping tens
and twenties into the *C* and *D* partitions of a stairwell bucket?
Can I get a vowel? I whispered to the bathroom ceiling
in Max Fish. Mr. Andrew Jackson rolled into a tight
green telescope, where whole swaths of the universe
became visible for an instant before splintering
into dark confetti. What was I thinking? My soul
a cash register stuffed with fake bills and subway tokens.
Miracle Legion cooing from the HiFi as we sniffed lines
off the Bowie coke mirror and chattered about all the art
we'd make. Bags of cotton candy detonating in our brains.
Was that thinking? Smearing globs of paint—magenta
bathing suits—over nude Polaroids. Now I know forever
what is behind Door Number Three: tiny plastic pieces
from the game Risk bobbing jagged in my bloodstream,
wincing as glints of sunlight knife through the slatted blinds,
the world: a black-and-white television set with three channels.
What do I think about that summer? It felt three miles
north of good: Mardi Gras in the blood, a mashed dragon's tail
in a hot dog bun. But it left me an alley cat in the tallest
branches of a pine, gnawing my own fur, my brain
pressed inward by a potter's hands, but also pressing out
like a fist. I think I stuck my head into the mouth of a dragon
and pulled it out in the nick of time from his guillotine lips.
Certainly I was a cad who chewed his cud. Certainly
I was a singed cod swimming in toilet water, ceding
chunks of his spirit, till all that was left was this scrap,
this gorgeous, pulsing scrap.

THE 6TH DAY OF THE 11TH MONTH

You're in shorts. Burning logs in a bronze tub radiate your legs.
Mars stares down at you with its yellowish-red eye.

Earlier you raked leaves, as the sunlight dragged it golden cape
west over coal factories in the Heartland, then turned the Grand Canyon

pink, and now sweeps the Pacific, where families in Malibu
huddle on sand, watching the last threads of gold

vanish into the undulating purple and black. South of here,
a man with orange skin sags, halfway between the ceiling

and a tray of French fries. He is both a bloated bag
of microwave popcorn and a deflating party balloon,

his little white string dangling limply. His dim offspring
draw straws to see who will break the news,

like an empty champagne bottle, over his head. In dark corridors
his ghoulish henchmen whisper about unsold tickets

to the clown show. They will skulk out of town
before dawn, their hands forever stained by the gussied-up

Brillo pads they passed off as cotton candy. Watch
the closing doors. Next stop: the wrong side of history.

Suddenly the flame in the bronze pit is the same color as Mars,
yet also a phoenix. The rebirth of democracy? Ok, a little much.

But didn't something just rise from the ashes, the dirt,
the cellar, its veins flickering skinny ropes of fire?

COLD OUT

It's so cold, the moon
ducks inside a cloud
to look for earmuffs.

If I were water,
my pants would be a tray
and my legs would be ice.

It's so cold, a cat lurks
under a car looking for
the echo of engine warmth.

Even the dog,
who has a coat
built into his body,

wears a knitted vest
as he sniffs for the toilet
hiding in the bushes.

A man walks by,
the loneliest thermometer
in his corduroys.

Later he will ask his wife
can I take your temperature
and she will say *not tonight,*

and tuck her battery-powered
thermometer under the pillow
and blow out the lights.

THIEF OF TWILIGHT

Thief of twilight, windpipe chiseler,
dripping onto the lips, almost tipsy,
then napping like a vagrant in the sinuses
for days. Only to wake and sandpaper
the taste buds, slide down
the trachea's flagpole, spray paint
mucus on the lungs. *Mercy*, we whimper
at the sky, but still you come, vandal,
with your overnight bag, scissors,
and oxygen straw, taping silver dollars
over the eyelids of people we love.

SHOVELING AT MIDNIGHT IN PAJAMAS

Twenty-six degrees. That's thirteen times two.
It's mid–December and already God
is pulling down his pants and waving
his holy ice pick in our faces. *Hello, sunshine,*
you mutter as the moon peeks over a wall
of clouds. A pine tree reaches above
a neighbor's chimney. A stray cat licks
its paws under a parked truck. The places
we go for a little warmth. That is
what defines us. All the trash we chase,
ripping through advice like papier-mâché
to feel: the hands of strangers, attention
we didn't get as kids, clumps of weed,
a line of gunpowder. Nothing will stop us.
You see it all so clearly—then it's gone,
your thirty-second enlightenment.
And your back in your driveway, shovel
in hand. The oak tree welcoming you
with brittle, empty arms.

SEX TOYS OF THE FUTURE

We met in a parking lot.
She handed me an envelope.
It's a map of my psyche, she said.
Take this, I said, handing her a green pill.
It's a history of my childhood.

I'm too tired to have sex tonight,
she yawned. *Can you do it
with my hologram instead?*

Sure, I said, reaching under the bed.
I grabbed her vibrator,
and unscrewed the top.
It doubled as a burrito microwave.

Let's just have the clones do it, I said,
igniting my infrared toothbrush.
Kinky or vanilla, she asked, looking up
from the screen built-into her palm.

Let's put them on fuck-till-you-die mode,
have them do it standing in the flower bed,
and we can fall asleep to the savage
futuristic music of our youth.

these are the things I can do without

In the other room,
the dentist talks
about the barbecue
that didn't happen,
the golf game
that did. In the small
room of my mouth,
another tooth
throbs in its death bed.
The other teeth
gather around:
good-bye, mister
molar, it's been real.
In the curved room
of my ear, a Tears
for Fears song
unspools. *Shout,*
shout. In the room
behind my eyes,
an old woman sits
alone in a chair,
applying makeup
in the dark.

Miss Trauma Shoulders

Timber, she hissed with a smile,
Her tongue: a tender chainsaw.
Who stuck the teddy bear in the microwave?
Who shaved the eyebrow of the hurricane?
Let my fingers do the walking
     over the cobblestones of your spine.
Let the blue of the sky be bottled
     and sold by the pint.
Let's use the Pleiades for target practice.
Constellations popping like light bulbs.
Let me hammer a kiss into your forehead.
Let me rub the death back into your metacarpals,
     Miss Trauma Shoulders.
Let me tug down your lower lip
     like a priest's red boxers.
Your teeth: tiny white Bibles
     sinking their holy truth into me.

Dad Museum

"You work and live in a room filled with your dead father's
memories," my wife says as I lean over to write, the desk

bracketed by plastic bins of framed photographs
and fifty-year-old family memorabilia. This is the summer

of building obstacle courses between me and the blank page.
Last night Saturn and Jupiter were hanging

just to the right of the moon, and I understood for a moment
what John Donne was asking God for in *The Holy Sonnets,*

but none of this is what I wanted to write about. I was in the car
with my fourteen-year-old and her three friends, driving them

to the city. After a dad joke belly-flopped. I adjusted
the rearview to avoid all eye contact. I felt like a washed-up shoe

on a beach no one goes to, a shoe people last wore
in the nineties. We glided down the Palisades, hit the GW Bridge.

The skyline erupted in the distance. The first bars
of Jay-Z's *Empire State of Mind* thumped from the speakers.

This city, a modern day Pompei, that took such a beating
for fifteen months, shook off the ref and staggered

back to its feet. This city of moxie and glitter
that animates the spirit, and volcanic ash that preserves

the multitudes of moments we have lived. Me at eight
with my dad in nineteenth-century costumes

in the Empire State Building photo booth, my dirt-bound dad
whose possessions surround me now in my studio. Me at fifteen:

a stoned day-tripper from Philly, conned at Three-card Monte
in Times Square. Seventeen: in Danceteria, my earrings

shimmering in the club's bionic light. Twenty: underwear-bathing
at dawn with two Mingus-haired nymphs in a Midtown high-rise

rooftop pool. Twenty-two, -three, -four, -five prowling
the midnight Alphabet streets in a red tank top and a scowl,

copping postage-stamp baggies of crushed Saturn. Twenty-six:
four days clean, praying in the Nuyorican bathroom

just before hitting the mic. Thirty-four: the giant Walkie-Talkies
vaporized before my eyes. Forty-four: ducking

under a jungle gym during a flash summer thunderstorm,
my daughter's hand: a warm, pulsing jewel in mine. Her three friends

and her ate drunken noodles and roamed the High Line.
What we think is our life often turns out to be a snow globe

in someone else's fist. But what do I know? I'm just a bad son
who tried to make up for it by turning his studio into a dad museum.

THE GLASS OF MILK

There is a glass of milk on a wooden table.
Inside the glass of milk: a tiny man
    with a scuba mask on.
Inside the tiny man's stomach: an even tinier hamburger.
Inside the tiny hamburger: a gigantic *mooo*, a century of pain.
Inside the century of pain: file cabinets
    filled with bruises and eviction notices and photos.
Inside one of the photos: a glass of milk
    on a wooden table.
Inside the glass of milk: a tiny cow, saying *this is my milk,
    motherfucker. You better not drink it.*
Inside the tiny cow: a tiny cheeseburger in a paper bag
    with an eviction notice disguised as lettuce.
Inside the eviction notice: the name of a family
    that must be out by morning.
Inside the family: a silence, as the father drops
    a lit cigarette into a glass of milk.

CREIGH

Hair so blonde, almost white.
Knocking pizza boxes from the hands
of grown-ups. Eyes so cold and blue
like they were kept in a freezer.
It's always the little ones
with Roman candles for limbs,
lighting firecrackers on street corners,
ripping antennas off parked cars,
igniting that crack rock like the one candle
on the devil's birthday cake.
Always the little ones.
No patience for sports, but fast as buckshot,
running quicksilver up drainpipes.
A bloodhound's nose for trouble.
High school girls at Ted Nugent concerts
pulling his twelve-year-old twinkle
into their cotton candy breasts.
Carrying a bullet fragment in his stomach
like a miniature lead infant.
Lifting back from the dead like Lazarus.
Look at him now, in a dark blue suit,
his nine cat lives tucked in his sock.
Parents in the front row, eyes foggy
portholes of grief. Five ex-girlfriends
spread across the room, like stakes
holding up the tent of his mythology.
His name tattooed on a married woman's hip,
and me up here—Mister Eulogy, talking around
Sherriff Joe's Tent City and Graterford Prison—
shining a flashlight onto the bullet hole
and calling it a third eye.

Aftermath of Hurricane Ida

You're standing in water up to your knees.
You're not in the basement.
Your house is not flooded.
You've driven twenty-six hundred miles the last six days.
You're at Rye Town Beach, the first Tuesday in September.
The sun is not a yellow motorboat.
The sun is not an egg cracking over your skull's porcelain bowl.
You're in the water, looking back at several hundred people
        scattered across a sickle of sand.
The swells of the estuary splash up your calves.
From this distance, the people look like specks
        in a pointillist painting.
One of the specks is your daughter, adjusting her goggles,
        about to enter the piranha tank of tenth grade.
You look down at your fifty-four-year-old hands.
Ten measly fingers and two palms.
A classroom of tiny white fish flicker by your ankles.
You dip your knuckles into the ripple.
How little we can help the ones we love.

THIS WEEK

This week I planted three diabetes pills in the backyard
    and they grew into Coca-Cola bottles.

This week part of a tooth declared mutiny and crumbled
    into a soup dumpling from Flushing, Queens.

This week I let the wind into my blouse and we went to second base.

This week a spy in China watched me masturbate
    to a Playboy centerfold from 1753.

This week I filled my pillow with credit card bills and dreamed
    about the claws of time.

I was filmed by forty-seven different hidden cameras.

I did the dishes hard and fast on the kitchen's granite counter
    while my wife watched a comedy in the other room.
    I licked maple syrup off a fork and whispered
    who's your daddy into a chipped coffee cup.

This week I failed six different tests, on six different chessboards.

This week I said *no more* to the sandpaper underpants
    and then an hour later I stapled on the sandpaper underpants.

This week, and it's only Tuesday.

Tomorrow

A girlfriend in college had body parts
        under her bed.
Her father worked in construction.
Can I lend you a hand, she joked,
the world is ending tomorrow.

On a shelf, she had an aquarium
where the penises of all the men
        she'd slept with
floated like bloated needlefish.

On some other planet, there's a museum,
showcasing every hand you ever shook.
A history of your life in touch.
But it doesn't matter
because the world is ending tomorrow.

Good-bye crooked lamp.
Good-bye wilting plant I shoved in the backseat
        from my father's Delaware funeral.
Good-bye Earl Grey tea and Yunnan Golden Tips.
Good-bye monthly archipelago of bills.
Good-bye twenty-two-pound puppy
        who I pulled to my chest at dawn.
Good-bye wife who has endured the many birds
        of my personality.
Come here, little critter, little friend, little bee.
Let the four of us hold each other on the living room floor
        and feel the heat lamps of each other's chests
        because the world is ending tomorrow.

Vesper for DP

The geese are flying back from the south in a broken V,
or are they carrying the spirit of a friend? Hard to say now.

We're all trying to hold it together. All of us
with our broken alphabet. Damaged bumpers.

Chipped mugs. But still we sing and flap our wings
and look down at the world we left behind,

the world we're coming back to. A man on a bicycle
pedals by with an empty child seat. Sir, you've lost your child,

we mumble. Why are you coming back to this, we ask
the geese. Don't you know our friend is gone?

Don't you know this town is grieving? A small plane
rumbles across the sky, dangling a fishhook

covered in breadcrumbs. The plane is fishing for birds.
The sky is an aquarium. And we are here on the bottom

of the tank, walking our dogs through the water
that we breathe. We see our friend blindfolded, carrying

a candle in the dark, inching across the iced-over Hudson,
as if a thousand frozen hands are holding him up,

and the ice breaks and he sinks peacefully into the world
beneath this one, where Jamaican cab drivers

give life advice and the gelato is always free. We remember
his love of quality mustards and charcuterie. The flash

of tenderness in his eyes. The pinball game
behind his sockets. A wad of two-dollar bills in his pocket.

Batman in the kitchen making spider sauce.
How, when we went north-south, he shined

east-west. An architect of filthy jokes
built plank by audacious plank. How he'd find

a dark fuse in the conversation and light it and smile,
a fishhook sparkling between his teeth. And still the geese

drag that broken V across the sky. V is for *velvet,*
for *violet,* for *vein,* for *vesper.* His spirit all around us

like a vanilla mist, here in our bruised valley,
the mist snickering: *hey, you jive turkeys.*

Thin Ice Olympics

Three miles in and already
the lane departure warning has beeped
four times. *Please take a break* blinks
in orange letters. Falling water frozen
on a rock formation. Forty miles to go.

★

We asked autumn if it could break a dollar.
It changed the bill into coins, the green leaves
into crinkly brown–boot fodder,
but nothing changed for us.
Masks are worn every season.

★

You peer at the eyes of parents
at the local farmers market and wonder
which one is next.

★

A few dads feel built for this moment.
This is the crisis they've been waiting for.
The increased threat of death is the stone
against which their focus sharpens.
They transition to indoor exercise.
Mass anxiety: a kind of fuel.

★

You see a dad on the ice, doing card tricks
as he skates blindfolded. *The ice looks as thin
as a glass credit card*, you want to say,
but instead you just wave hi neighbor.

★

A figure skater twirls on the frozen river.
The thermometer creeps up into the forties.
Her blades Ginsu the ice as she gathers speed
for the triple axel. She lands and the glass
dissolves and she vanishes like a sparkly
purple exclamation mark into the dark current.

*

Our metaphorical ice is thinner.
We're all snorting paint thinner.
Instead of a Tchaikovsky soundtrack
and a purple tutu, we're in pajamas
listening to the ragged music
of our own breathing. The floorboards
quiver under our dirty socks.

*

We will debate for decades which was worse:
illness or cure. We will retroactively cobble
together statistics, looking for the pieces
of a thousand ripped-up photographs
flung into the ocean.

*

One of the photos is of a stay-at-home dad
who went so deep into a psychedelic rabbit hole
that his very eyes became rabbit holes in his face.
One midnight, in that wretched seasonal corridor,
that February serpentine before spring, he mixed
a thimble of arsenic into a raspberry smoothie.

*

We are all so isolated and packed in together.
That was a loving dad who plummeted through
the domestic ice. The Olympics
is just surviving. And what of your ice?
This February, it's different, isn't it? A family you love,
a dad pulling rabbits from a hat. And poof.
A black hat on the ice where he'd been standing.

You keep expecting him to pull himself out.

Notes

This book is arranged mostly in the order that the poems were written,
beginning in the summer of 2019 and ending in the spring of 2022.
A few poems have been moved within the year they were written.
"Pandemic Parable" is the only poem to jump years. It was the final piece
written in June 2022.

Covid slammed New York City and the surrounding areas in mid-March
2020, before reverberating through the rest of the country.

The childhood friends referenced in "November Red-Eye…" are Drew
O'Leary and Creigh Horvath. (It should be noted that after taking that
red-eye, my daughter, Camilla, dropped twenty-seven points in an eighth
grade CYO game.)

The first draft of "Notes on Miro's *The Birth of the World*" was written at
the MOMA, December 2019.

"When the Cat's Away". The phrase *"Little thieves are hanged, but big thieves
escape"* is a variation of a Russian proverb. A paddy wagon is a police van.

"The Haber Process" refers to the Texas City disaster, an industrial
accident in 1947, that killed at least 581 people, including all but one
member of the Texas City volunteer fire department.

In May 2020, there were a trio of national racial events. The first was the
video leak of the murder of Ahmaud Arbery, who was killed while
jogging. The murder happened several months before, but the video,
filmed by one of the white attackers, was not released until May 5th. May
25th began with the Central Park birdwatching incident video, filmed by
Christian Cooper, and ended the with the murder of George Floyd in
Minneapolis. I wrote and discarded several poems trying to address
racism and white privilege. "Facts" is all that remains.

"Beige Hero(in) July". Max Fish was a bar in the Lower East Side in the
'90s known for its cool jukebox and the privacy of its bathrooms.

"Vespers for DP" is for David Poses.

ACKNOWLEDGMENTS

Thank you B O D Y, *Girl Blood Info*, and *The Best of Write Bloody Publishing Anthology* for printing several of the poems contained here.

Thank you Amy Gerstler for reading several versions of this manuscript and giving infrared feedback, illuminating a path forward, from beginning to end.

Thank you Julia Edwards for reading the manuscript and giving invaluable feedback, and then detailed editorial notes in the home stretch, helping shepherd the book over the finish line.

Thank you to the 24—Julia Edwards, Rhoni Blankenhorn, Claire Denson, and Chessy Normile—where many first drafts from this book were first posted.

Thank you Sarah Koskoff for allowing me to sit in on your generative workshop in the fall of 2021, where a handful of these poems emerged.

Thank you Derrick Brown for publishing the book. Who would have thunk it when we met twenty-six years ago at a reading in a coffee shop in Long Beach, California?

Thank you Nikki Steele and the rest of the Write Bloody team for your tireless work.

Thank you Angelo Maneage for the excellent cover designs.

Thank you Kendra DeColo for the bang-up, three-dimensional editing job.

Thank you Alex Wolfe for the fine-tooth comb.

Thank you Alida Bradenburg and Eleni Angelopoulos for allowing me to read out loud an earlier incarnation of this book over the phone.

Thank you Christine and Camilla and Levi for sharing the pandemic with me. The best quarantine crew ever.

Thank you Caroline Kaye for the excellent photo.

Thank you to the fire pit crew: Ivy, Bekah, Courtney, Richard, and Christine.

Thank you to the Peeps. And the Core. You know who you are.

Thank you Joan Wasser for the blurb and nineteen years of friendship.

Thank you for the love of friends: Alex, Sarah, Todd, Ivy, Amy, John, Paisley, Terrance and others.

Thank you to the poetry communities that nurtured me in my formative years: Sarah Lawrence undergrad (the Badger/Beef Kabob years); GMU MFA (Cindy Goff, Greg Grummer, Chuck Fox, Mannal, Poetry Theater); DC WritersCorps/Black Cat Club (Kenny Carroll, DJ Renegade, Brian Gilmore, Silvana Straw, Jose Padua, Joe Ray Sandoval, Stephen Gibson); Los Angeles/Beyond Baroque (Ellyn Maybe, Aimee Bender, Derrick Brown, the Dead Poets Slam, Venice Beach Slam Team); and the global spoken word community (Beth Lisick, Justin Chin, Matt Cook, Rayl and Ko in Munich, Marc Smith, the Nuyorican Poets Café, Keith Roach, Sean Thomas Dougherty, and so many others).

Thank you Christine for keeping the wheels on the proverbial bus and for your fantastic, high-wire work behind the scenes, bringing this book to fruition.

Thank you Camilla for being such an inspiration. Watching you navigate the pandemic and other challenges with such grace amazes me. And thank you for teaching me the meaning of Arc.

And eternal gratitude to my mentor Thomas Lux. Yes, they gave me a uniform.

About the Author

Jeffrey McDaniel is the author of six previous books of poetry, most recently *Holiday in the Islands of Grief* (University of Pittsburgh Press, 2020). Other books include *Chapel of Inadvertent Joy* (Pittsburgh, 2013), *The Endarkenment* (Pittsburgh, 2008), *The Splinter Factory* (Manic D Press, 2002), *The Forgiveness Parade* (Manic D, 1998), and *Alibi School* (Manic D, 1995). McDaniel's poems have appeared in numerous places, including *The New Yorker, American Poetry Review, The New York Times,* and *Best American Poetry 1994, 2010,* and *2019.* A recipient of an NEA Fellowship, he teaches at Sarah Lawrence College and lives in the Hudson Valley.

If You Like Jeffrey McDaniel, Jeffrey Likes…

Every Little Vanishing by Sheleen McElhenney

No Matter the Wreckage by Sarah Kay

Open Your Mouth Like a Bell by Mindy Nettifee

Racing Hummingbirds by Jeanann Verlee

1000 Black Umbrellas by Daniel McGinn

Write Bloody Publishing publishes and promotes great books of poetry every year. We believe that poetry can change the world for the better. We are an independent press dedicated to quality literature and book design, with an office in Los Angeles, California. We are grassroots, DIY, indie, diversity power believers. Pull up a good book and join the family. Support independent authors, artists, and presses. Want to know more about Write Bloody books, authors, and events?

www.writebloody.com

WRITE BLOODY BOOKS

After the Witch Hunt — Megan Falley

Aim for the Head: An Anthology of Zombie Poetry — Rob Sturma, Editor

Allow The Light: The Lost Poems of Jack McCarthy — Jessica Lohafer, Editor

Amulet — Jason Bayani

Any Psalm You Want — Khary Jackson

Atrophy — Jackson Burgess

Birthday Girl with Possum — Brendan Constantine

The Bones Below — Sierra DeMulder

Born in the Year of the Butterfly Knife — Derrick C. Brown

Bouquet of Red Flags — Taylor Mali

Bring Down the Chandeliers — Tara Hardy

Ceremony for the Choking Ghost — Karen Finneyfrock

A Constellation of Half-Lives — Seema Reza

Counting Descent — Clint Smith

Courage: Daring Poems for Gutsy Girls — Karen Finneyfrock,
Mindy Nettifee, & Rachel McKibbens, Editors

Cut to Bloom — Arhm Choi Wild

Dear Future Boyfriend — Cristin O'Keefe Aptowicz

Do Not Bring Him Water — Caitlin Scarano

Don't Smell the Floss — Matty Byloos

Drive Here and Devastate Me — Megan Falley

Drunks and Other Poems of Recovery — Jack McCarthy

The Elephant Engine High Dive Revival — Derrick C. Brown, Editor

Every Little Vanishing — Sheleen McElhinney

Everyone I Love Is a Stranger to Someone — Annelyse Gelman

Everything Is Everything — Cristin O'Keefe Aptowicz

Favorite Daughter — Nancy Huang

The Feather Room — Anis Mojgani

Floating, Brilliant, Gone — Franny Choi